Contents

A RIVER, a **Flood**, and **Lots** of **SAND**
... **Just What We Need** to Build a Civilization

Welcome to Egypt!

What do you know about ancient Egypt?
Probably that the pharaohs built the pyramids.
Or that they turned their dead into mummies.
Or that they wrote in hieroglyphs. Correct?

Well, none of that is WRONG, but it's only PART of the story. We're going to take you behind the scenes.

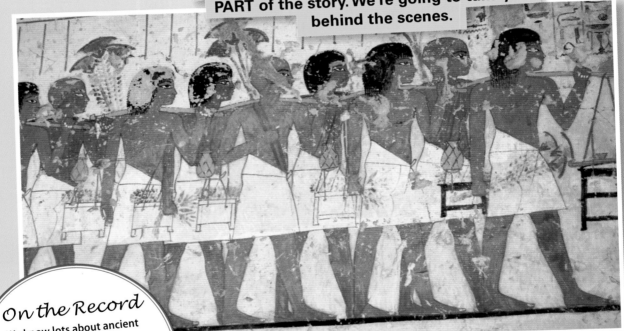

On the Record
We know lots about ancient Egypt. The Egyptians had three different ways of writing, and kept careful records. These accounts are carved into stone or written on a kind of paper called papyrus.

The ancient Egyptian civilization lasted for over 3,000 years. That's far longer than the time that has passed from the end of the civilization until now. A lot happened in such a long period. Rulers rose and fell. Different parts of the country became more or less important. But many parts of Egyptian life were very stable. Their beliefs, culture and daily life didn't change much.

BAS 11/16

...in history

WAYLAND

www.waylandbooks.co.uk

This paperback edition first published in Great Britain in 2016 by Wayland

Wayland
An imprint of Hachette Children's Group
Part of Hodder & Stoughton
Carmelite House
50 Victoria Embankment
London EC4Y 0DZ
An Hachette UK Company
www.hachette.co.uk
www.hachette-childrens.co.uk

ISBN: 978 0 7502 8964 1

Brown Bear Books Ltd.
First Floor
9–17 St. Albans Place
London
N1 0NX

Author: Tim Cooke
Designer: Lynne Lennon
Picture manager: Sophie Mortimer
Design manager: Keith Davis
Editorial director: Lindsey Lowe
Children's publisher: Anne O'Daly

Printed in China

Websites

The website addresses (URLs) included in this book were valid at the time of going to press. However, because of the nature of the internet, it is possible that some addresses may have changed, or sites may have changed or closed down since publication. While the author and publisher regret any inconvenience this may cause the readers, no responsibility for any such changes can be accepted by either the author or the publisher.

Picture credits

Key: b = bottom, bgr = background, c = centre, is = insert, l = left, mtg = montage, r = right, t = top.

Front Cover: All images **Shutterstock.**
Interior: Alamy: AF Archive 27; **Bridgeman Art Library:** Louvre/Giraudon 20, Dreamstime: 15cr; **Getty Images:** Richard Nowitz/National Geographic 9br; **Shutterstock:** 6l, 7, 12, 19t, 22, 28, Arthur R. 6br, BasPhoto 13t, Ryan M. Bolton 25b, Dan Breckwoldt 5b, JSP 22–23b, Anthony Jackson 26, Pius Lee 16, Mario Lopes 15cr, Mare and Mare 8, Mountainpix 21br, John Michael Evan Potter 17cl, Jeff Schultz 15t, Michiel de Witt 15b, Gubin Yury 25tr; **Thinkstock:** Hemera 21t, istockphoto 1b,4, 5t, 9l, 10, 11, 14, 24; Photos.com 13bl, 19b, 23, 29.

All other artworks Brown Bear Books.

Brown Bear Books has made every attempt to contact the copyright holder. If you have any information please contact licensing@brownbearbooks.co.uk

KINGDOM ON THE NILE

- Ancient Egypt had two main parts: Lower Egypt was a delta at the mouth of the Nile; Upper Egypt was a narrow valley through which the river runs.
- The two parts of Egypt were united in 3150 B.C.E. under King Narmer.
- The Egyptians were ruled by kings and queens called pharaohs.
- Some rulers came from places outside Egypt, such as Nubia, Libya or Greece.
- In 30 B.C.E. Egypt became a province of ancient Rome, ending the civilization.

Hot facts

★ **Egyptian** history is divided into kingdoms and periods.

★ **The Old Kingdom** lasted from 2650 to 2150 B.C.E. The Middle Kingdom lasted from 2000 to 1700 B.C.E. The New Kingdom was from 1550 to 1070 B.C.E.

★ **The kingdoms** were settled periods when power passed peacefully from ruler to ruler; a sequence of rulers who are related in some way is called a dynasty.

★ **The periods**, or time between the kingdoms, were less settled. Egypt was divided by civil war among dynasties or by foreign invasion.

huge tombs for kings

The Great Pyramid at Giza was the tallest building on Earth for over 4,000 years.

Grand DESIGNS

If there's one thing Egyptians are really good at, it's building things. Not just the mudbrick houses most of us live in – they're quite ordinary. But think about the huge stone structures we build for our gods and kings? They're out of this world!

Is it **Meant to** look like **That?**

Oh dear. We hear that King Snefru is looking very unhappy. His attempt to be the first ruler to build a smooth-sided pyramid has ended in disaster.

The angle of the walls was so steep the whole thing was likely to collapse. At the last minute, the builders changed the pitch of the slope. So Snefru still got his pyramid – but everyone says it looks bent!

ONE STEP AHEAD

Yet again, King Djoser is one step ahead of everyone else. The trend-setting king has built himself a huge burial mound. It rises like a giant four-sided stairway to heaven. Each level has a smaller level on top. Djoser calls this a pyramid. It's the tallest building anyone has ever seen. Let's hope it fulfils the king's wish to get closer to Amun-Re, the sun-god.

Bonkers building: What a building **BOOM** – the pharaohs have built more than 100 pyramids

Rulers' graves
There are three tall pyramids at Giza, and three smaller queens' pyramids.

Khufu builds himself the tallest pyramid!

Optical trick
The pyramid on the right is the Great Pyramid. The middle one just looks bigger.

mine is **bigger than** yours

This is getting out of control! It all started with Djoser and Snefru. Now every king wants his own pyramid, and also pyramids for his queens and officials.

Pharaoh Khufu is going higher than anyone else with his Great Pyramid at Giza. At 150 metres (490 ft) high, it will take 80,000 workers at least five years to build. As usual, a whole village will have to be created for the builders. They will have to quarry and polish about 2.3 million limestone blocks and drag them to Giza. Each block weighs as much as 15 tonnes (16.5 t).

A **Heavenly Home**

There's only one rule when it comes to gods' homes: the bigger, the better. With so many gods, we need lots of temples for them to live in.

The temples are huge, with gateways, enclosures and great halls. We fill the temples with lovely statues of the gods as gifts, to show the gods we love them. A priest makes daily offerings of food and incense.

Builder for **Hire**

If you want to build something big, hire Imhotep. He's got a great CV. He designed Djoser's step-pyramid at Saqqara, the first big stone building anywhere in the world. It helps that Imhotep is a genius at maths. The pyramid has four equal sides that meet in a point right in the middle! But hire him while he's still alive – he's bound to be made a god when he dies.

✔ Use **LIMESTONE** to make the sides of pyramids **GLEAMING** white!

Funky Pharaohs

Pharaohs rule all of Egypt. They pass the throne from father to son in a royal line, or dynasty. But to hold on to their thrones, the kings have to keep the gods happy – which is easier said than done.

Double crown
Ramesses II wears a double crown to symbolise the union of Upper and Lower Egypt.

False beard
Pharaohs wore false beards, because beards were associated with the gods.

Takes one to know one

Not many Egyptians ever get to see the pharaoh. But if you do, remember that the pharaoh is a god (and his wife is a goddess). That's why we worship him. The pharaoh's job is to keep the other gods happy. In return they make sure the River Nile floods every year, so the farmers can grow enough food for everyone.

Cartouche
This symbol identifies the statue as Ramesses.

Pharaoh manual: ✔ Get **MORE NAMES!** New Kingdom pharaohs have three different names.

PASSING ON POWER

Pharaohs like to pass the throne on to their sons or brothers – even their wives. The period a single family holds power is called a dynasty. Some dynasties have lasted for 14 kings. There have been 31 dynasties in all. We keep track by grouping them into three kingdoms and three intermediate periods.

Jog On, Pharaoh!

Are you going to Heb Sed? This royal jubilee comes after a pharaoh has ruled for 30 years. Wearing a kilt with an animal's tail, he has to run round a ritual course four times. It's meant to show he's still healthy and fit to rule. But we hear he'll have a rest during the parades that follow the run.

Seven Top Kings

Osiris the first ruler of Egypt (although some say he was only a myth)

Narmer/Menes (1st Dynasty) the first Egyptian king we're sure existed

Khufu (4th Dynasty) put Egypt on the map with his Great Pyramid

Hatshepsut (18th Dynasty) queen for 20 years. She ruled dressed as a man!

Akhenaten (18th Dynasty) unpopular because he got rid of all gods except the sun god and built a new capital. It was abandoned after he died.

Tutankhamun (18th Dynasty) The son of Akhenaten was the first boy-racer king. He died as a teenager after a chariot accident.

Ramesses II (19th Dynasty) known as Ramesses the Great because he ruled for 67 years. He built more statues and monuments than any other pharaoh.

King's portrait looks too real

Funny face
Akhenaten was a rebel king. Even his statue looks different from other kings.

 Carry a big **STICK**! Called a sceptre, this is a sign of authority. Don't forget your **CROWN** in public.

9

A **trip along** the *River Nile*

Egypt wouldn't be here if it wasn't for the River Nile. It's a water supply, it irrigates our crops and it's a highway. It's full of fish for food (and crocodiles that might turn *you* into food). Away from the Nile 90 per cent of Egypt is sand, nothing but sand…

One direction
The Nile flows from south to north; it made it easy to travel the length of Egypt.

Highway Code ✓

If you want to get anywhere quickly, head for the river. (Wheels haven't been invented yet – and they'd get stuck in the sand, anyway.) Travel by boat. There are papyrus canoes for short trips and wooden sailing boats for longer journeys.

Most captains use sails to travel upstream, then row back down with the current. You probably won't be alone. Boats carry passengers and all sorts of cargo, from animal sacrifices for temples to fish for supper!

City guide: Check out Egypt's greatest **CITIES**: Alexandria Heliopolis Memphis Saqqara

Cataracts

If you're going further than Aswan, near the southern border of the kingdom, hire a good captain to sail your boat. To the south, the Nile runs through rapids known as cataracts. It's easy to capsize, so most travellers don't risk it.

Travel WARNING ❌

Travellers on the Nile should use great caution between June and October. That's the time of the inundation, or annual flood, when the river overflows its banks. Of course, if you're not travelling, the inundation is a good thing. It covers a strip of land with thick silt from upstream. This *Keme*, or Black Land, is where we grow our crops.

Fancy tool

A Nilometer can be a simple hole in the ground, or something more ornate.

Nilometers ✓

For the latest in water technology, visit Elephantine Island near Aswan. This 'Nilometer' measures the height of the river. It has steps sunk down to the water, so it's a more accurate way of measuring water levels than the old stone columns with depth markers on the side. The government records the flood levels each year. A flood of 14 *ells* is ideal (an ell is 1.5 metres/4.9 feet), but anything over 18 ells is a disaster. The water might wash away towns along the river.

Keeping up
Appearances

Everyone wants to look good. Anyone who can afford it wears make-up and wigs when they go out, and linen is the favoured fabric. The softest linen is kept for the pharaoh.

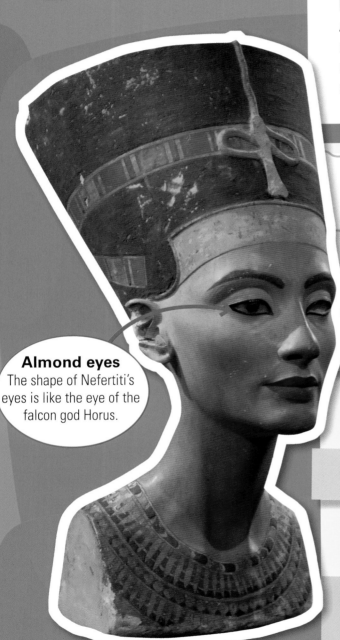

Almond eyes
The shape of Nefertiti's eyes is like the eye of the falcon god Horus.

Nefertiti's make-up **Tips**

Nefertiti, the queen of Pharaoh Akhenaten, is a famous Egyptian beauty. We asked her for her beauty secrets.

★ To make my eyes look bigger and wide-awake, I use eye paint. The best ones are made from ground-up minerals.

★ Lead sulfide, or kohl, gives a grey-black colour. Malachite, or copper ore, makes green. Try using both at once. Gorgeous!

★ Use iron powder to make your cheeks and lips a healthy-looking red.

★ If you find your make-up powder is dry, try mixing it with some melted animal fat. That'll make it much easier to apply.

★ Get yourself a good palette. Make sure it has a smooth dish to grind your make-up.

Makeover magic: Remember – **BEAUTY** is a sign of **HOLINESS** – **MAKE-UP** is magic

How to **wear** YOUR **wig**

This new idea sounds crazy. Why shave off all your hair – and then wear a wig instead? According to fans, it's the only way to avoid head lice.

The best wigs are made from real human hair and held in place with beeswax. If that's too expensive, try a wig made from cheaper material such as wool or grass. Failing that, you could always just shave your head!

The problem with all these wigs is that everyone looks the same in their portraits!

Out of Fashion

Not everyone is interested in a fashionable life. Slaves and poor people wear loincloths made from coarse wool. They're good for working in, because they're cool and tougher than linen. But they are *SOooo* boring.

Perfect setting
Complement your make-up with sparkling gold and silver jewellery

Stylewatch

Luxurious Linen

Instead of new styles, fashion followers spend their money on luxurious fabrics (of course, the very best is for the pharaoh only). The most comfortable cloth is linen, woven from the fibres of flax plants. Men wear a linen kilt, while women usually make it into a tunic or a long, sheath-like dress.

See-through Chic

Take care with the finest linen. It's almost see through! To preserve your modesty, make sure your tunic has loads of fine pleats in the appropriate places. They'll thicken the appearance of the fabric.

White linen makes a great setting for lots and lots of bling: solid gold and precious jewels for the wealthy, and glass beads for the best of the rest.

 Too **MANLY** to wear **make-up**? This is **magical** protection! Everyone **NEEDS** it!

13

Food glorious *Food!*

Egyptians love to eat. Thanks to the fertile banks of the Nile, farmers can grow all kinds of crops, from figs and melons to cucumbers and onions. Few animals are bred for food – so meat is a real luxury.

Get Some Leverage
The longer the arm on a shaduf, the less effort you need to lift the water.

Well, well, well!

Farmer's Forecast

Here's the annual forecast for farmers. This year's Nile flood, or inundation, will begin in June and last until October – just like last year, and the year before that … and just like every year anyone can remember. That's the great thing about the inundation. It's reliable. Dig canals that will carry the flood water as far into the desert as possible. Once the flood has gone down, use a shaduf – a kind of bucket on a long pole with a counterweight – to lift water from the canals into the fields.

On the **Menu:** ✔ BREAD and BEER ✘ don't drink the WATER ✔ raw or dried FISH ✔ olive oil

Mind Your Teeth

Pharaoh Hatshepsut is complaining of toothache again. The royal advisers have found the answer. It's the fault of our daily flat bread. During the process of grinding the barley, grit and sand get into the flour. That's why we all have broken teeth – even the pharaohs!

Cheers!

Egyptians drink more beer than water! But it's not beer like you get in a pub. It's made by soaking bread in ale, so it's more like soup. To make it easier to drink, try straining it through a basket. (And of course, pubs haven't been invented – yet.)

Daily bread
Where would we be without bread? We rely on flat bread made from barley.

Hot party tips

Everyone loves a banquet, so our hospitality experts have come up with a few rules to guarantee your party goes with a swing!

1 ★ Clear your diary. Banquets can go on for hours, so be prepared for guests who just don't want to leave.

2 ★ Provide low couches so your guests of honour can lie down while they eat. Everyone else can just sit on the floor.

3 ★ Make sure there's enough bread. Lots and lots of bread. Other treats include wine, cakes and fruit.

4 ★ Fish from the Nile is always popular. Perch is great, but make sure it's fresh. It soon starts to smell unless you have preserved it in salt (in which case, remember to wash the salt off).

5 ★ Guests will eat with their fingers, so make sure your servants bring water so guests can wash their hands between courses.

6 ★ Many people can't afford meat, so even a little makes a meal special. Poultry, goat and lamb are popular. Or beef is a real treat (no wonder a man's wealth is measured by how many cattle he has).

✔ **FIGS**   ✔ **Honey**   ✘ Beef (too EXPENSIVE)   ✔ Raisins   ✔ More **BREAD**   ✔ Vegetables   ✔ **Wine**

Wildlife CORNER

It's a good idea to treat all animals with respect. It's true that Egypt is home to some pretty horrible species, like scorpions and jackals. But you never know – that animal might just be a god.

Dear Editors,

How come so many Egyptian gods look like animals?

A Confused Reader, Saqqara

Dear Confused of Saqqara,

We Egyptians have many gods. Because we don't know what they look like, we imagine them as humans with the heads of animals whose qualities they share. That's why the goddess of war, Sekhmet, has a lion's head – because lions are fierce. Anubis, the god of the dead, has a jackal's head. That's because jackals are often seen in necropolises, the big cemeteries outside our cities. Does that answer your question?

The SPHINX is said to be wiser than anyone on Earth

A GREAT GIZA

Everyone's heard of the Great Sphinx at Giza. It's the biggest statue in Egypt and probably in the world. The pharaoh's head has a lion's body to show that the pharaoh protects tombs and temples. But for a new kind of sphinx, try adding a falcon's head in honour of Horus. Or follow the example of Thebes. The Thebans have made 900 lions' bodies with rams' heads to show their devotion to the sheep-headed god Amon.

Cats and **Dogs**: which pet is better? Everyone has a **CAT** – they're **sacred**

Can't I WORSHIP a PUPPY?

Many animals are associated with the gods that control some of the more horrible parts of life – and death. The gods take the shape of some of the least pleasant of Egypt's creatures.

★ **JACKAL** – The jackal-headed god Anubis mummifies the dead. It's a very important job. Embalmers wear jackal masks while they turn dead bodies into mummies.

★ **DUNG BEETLE** – Kephri the beetle god rolls the sun through the heavens, like the scarab beetle rolling its ball of dung.

★ **CROCODILE** – Sobek the croc is the god of the Nile, where you always have to watch out for crocs in case they overturn your boat.

★ **SCORPION** – Serket the scorpion is the goddess of magic and she can easily punish any wrongdoers with her poisonous sting.

Mummified Cats

Cat lovers should head to Bubastis. The annual festival of Bastet, the cat-headed god, attracts more than 700,000 visitors. Cats are lucky, so many people keep them as pets. When your cat dies, remember to shave off your eyebrows as a sign of mourning. At Bubastis, special cemeteries hold many thousands of mummified cats. Everyone should try to visit at least once. Perhaps you should take Tiddles?

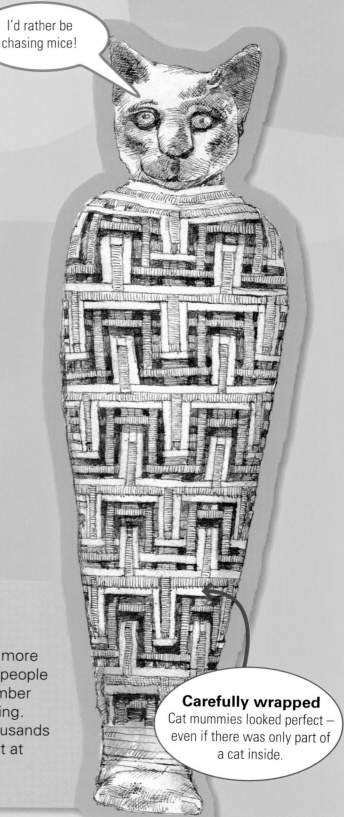

I'd rather be chasing mice!

Carefully wrapped
Cat mummies looked perfect – even if there was only part of a cat inside.

 Dogs GUARD houses at night ✖ **Cats** can't catch **DEER** ✖ **Dogs** are too fierce to allow indoors

Hanging **with** my *Mummy!*

As everyone knows, when you die you'll need your body in the Afterlife. That's why you need to preserve it by mummification. It's an expensive process, however – so it's only for the rich.

Take **Care** of your *Mummy*

'I couldn't have asked for better care for my father, Ramesses I'
Ramesses II (Pharaoh)

At Mummies4U we never forget that becoming a mummy is a once-in-a-lifetime experience. It's also an investment in your eternal future.

Our luxury service includes:

★ We make sure you are completely dead: you won't be mummified by accident.

★ We take your brain out without damaging your head. We'll use a long probe to mash it up and pull it out through your nose.

★ We remove your liver, lungs, stomach and intestines. We dry them, then put them back – you'll need them later!

★ We replace your real eyes with top-quality glass eyes so you can see in the next life.

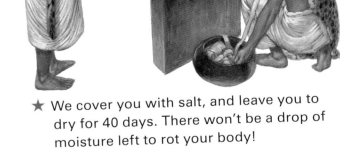

★ We cover you with salt, and leave you to dry for 40 days. There won't be a drop of moisture left to rot your body!

★ We guarantee never to touch the heart, so we don't disturb the soul that lives there.

Don't mind him – he's **dead!**: Mummies were buried in one or more **COFFINS**

What Bit Goes Where?

Here's a good way to stop your enemies using magic against you after you're dead. Once the embalmer has dried out your organs, get him to put them in canopic jars. There are different jars for the intestines, stomach, liver and lungs. But make sure he uses the right lids, so each organ is with the head of its correct guardian god. Otherwise the protection won't work so well.

DON'T FORGET THE GUIDEBOOK!

When you reach Duat, the Underworld, you'll find dangers like poisonous snakes and burning lakes. Help your dead soul avoid them by having spells painted in hieroglyphs on the walls of your tomb. For security, take papyrus scrolls of the spells in your coffin. These Books of the Dead will get you through Duat to Yaru, the Afterlife. What's it like there? It's just like this world, so you can carry on as before.

What happens...

When you die, you'll be off to the Hall of Two Truths, where the god Osiris will weigh your heart against a single feather.

... is in the balance

If your heart is lighter than the feather, you have lived a pure life. Thoth, the god of wisdom, will let you into the kingdom of Osiris. But if your heart is heavy, there's no Afterlife for you.

Don't get lost
All at sea in the Underworld? Don't worry – just follow the Book of the Dead.

 Important people were buried in house-like tombs called mastabas Poor people were just buried in holes in the ground

Queens of the NILE

I bathe in ass's milk to keep my skin soft.

Egypt might be called ancient, but in many ways it's quite modern. Take women. We're not like other ancient societies. Egyptian women can be doctors and priestesses. We can even be queens – or, er, kings.

Obituary of Cleopatra

We are sad to report the death of Egypt's famous queen, Cleopatra. She died after an accident with a poisonous snake called an asp.

She ruled from 51 to 30 B.C.E., making her the last ruler of ancient Egypt. She had love affairs with two Romans: Emperor Julius Caesar and his enemy, Mark Antony. Mark Antony was defeated in battle by Caesar's son. He killed himself. Now Cleopatra has done the same.

All Greek to me
Cleopatra was not Egyptian. The famous beauty was from a Greek dynasty.

TOP beauty in Egypt!

Women's rights: LADIES, you can: ✔ Own **property**, including **SLAVES** ✔ Make a **will**

Sisters are *Doing it* for **themselves!**

Nefertari

Nefertari was a favourite wife of Ramesses II, one of the greatest of all pharaohs. Her name means 'beautiful companion', and Ramesses built her the largest tomb in the Valley of the Queens. You can also see Nefertari on the front of the temple at Abu Simbel, along with her husband.

Nefertiti

Queen Nefertiti ruled with her husband, Akhenaten. They became unpopular when they banned the worship of all the old gods except the sun god, who they called Aten. After Akhenaten died, the worship of Aten became less important. The old gods were brought back and the sun god became just another deity.

Twosret

Another queen! Twosret ruled from 1187 to 1185 B.C.E., after the death of her husband Seti II and his heir, Siptah. She didn't have a good time – her reign ended in civil war and marked the end of the 19th Dynasty.

Meet *Pharaoh Hatshepsut*

Q. Pharaoh Hatshepsut, how do you think you've managed to stay in power for twenty years?
A. Well, it could be because the Egyptian economy is booming. We are at peace and trade has never been better. Look at all the temples I have built.

Q. And do you think it matters that you're a woman?
A. What do you mean?

Q. Well, you do dress in men's clothes. You even make people address you as 'king'. Isn't that a bit odd? Why do you do that?
A. If I'm a woman, that's my secret.

Q. With respect, it's not really a secret at all.
A. Really? Do you mean no-one is fooled by my false beard?

I thought I made a convincing man. Check out the false beard!

✔ Bring a **LEGAL** case against **anyone**　✖ Grow a **REAL** beard　✔ **Free a SLAVE**　✔ Adopt a **child**

Let's Go to WORK

The best job of all is to be pharaoh, but there is only one of those (or sometimes two, if competing dynasties rule different parts of the country). Of the other jobs available, some are better than others.

★★★ **Top Job** ★★ **Bearable** ★ **Oh Dear!**

Artist

There's plenty of work for artists, with so many tombs to decorate. Apprentices draw outlines in red, which senior artists correct in black. Painters colour in the outlines, using brushes of papyrus twine.

Scarecrow ★

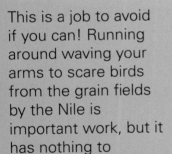

This is a job to avoid if you can! Running around waving your arms to scare birds from the grain fields by the Nile is important work, but it has nothing to recommend it. Your arms get tired and you get sunburned.

Farmer ★★

The fertile Nile mud and hot climate means farmers grow all kinds of crops: barley, emmer wheat, onions, garlic, dates, figs and lentils. Wealthy farmers have an ox to pull their plough. If you don't have an ox, you'll have to pull your plow by hand. Most farmers ask their wives and children to help!

Slave ★

A slave has no rights – so let's hope your owner is kind. If you live in a rich household, you should at least be fed well and have clothes to wear. Otherwise, you'll probably wear a loincloth and work in the fields. You might also have to help move huge stone blocks to build pyramids.

Scribe secrets: ✔ Scribes learn two scripts ✔ Hieroglyphs are a kind of picture writing

Embalmer ★ ★ ★

Being an embalmer is vital, as everyone needs their body in the next life. But this is not a job for the over-sensitive. Your clients are dead, so there's no conversation, and you have to be happy to remove their brains and cut out their organs. And you often have to do it all while wearing a jackal mask of the god Anubis. It gets hot inside there!

Scribble scribbler ★ ★ ★

If you want to be a scribe, start early. Boys start to study at nine (this isn't a job that girls can do). They train hard for five years, learning how to keep records and write letters for everyone – including the pharaoh, who can't read. It's hard work, but it has lots of perks. You're well paid, you don't pay taxes, you can be your own boss and you are always busy.

Setting out
People only become scribes after four or five years learning to write.

Harvest time
Working in the fields is tough, especially when the barley is ready to cut.

 They are slow to draw ✖ Hieroglyphs are used mainly for rituals ✔ Hieratic script is quicker to write, so has wider uses

Filling *SPARE time*

Hanging Out
Most of the hard work in Egypt is done by slaves. That means everyone else has quite a lot of spare time. Some people fill the time with hobbies. Others learn new skills, like maths.

Do you get bored easily? It often happens, as there are more than enough Egyptians to do the jobs that need doing. Here are suggestions for how you can fill any spare time.

Have you played senet? If you like backgammon, you'll love it. Two players move counters around a board divided into 30 squares that represent the soul's journey through the Underworld. One player represents the forces of evil and the other the forces of good. The pharaoh Tutankhamun loved senet so much, it was said he was buried with four sets of the game. Other people had themselves painted playing the game.

Another favourite game is snake. The stone board looks like a curled-up snake. The winner is the first person to move around the board to reach the centre.

A great **Toy** CHEST: ✔ Senet board and counters ✔ **SNAKE** board and counters ✔ Clay **BALLS** for catch

a **Royal** hobby

Everyone has plenty to eat, so no-one needs to hunt for food. Hunting is treated like a sport – but only the pharaoh and his court are allowed to take part. They hunt wild bulls, gazelles, antelopes, oryx (large antelope), lions and even hippos! To be honest, the whole thing is a bit of a cheat. Servants hunt down the poor animal on foot. Then the pharaoh goes in for the kill. But it's a good job most pharaohs have strong arms. They throw a spear or shoot a bow and arrow from the safety of their chariots.

Horrible hippo
Hippos were so dangerous they were thought to guard rivers in the Underworld.

You don't fight fair. Come over here and say that!

DO TELL TALES

Most Egyptians except scribes might not be able to read, but they still love a good story. They listen to professional storytellers who tell tales about the gods. One of our favourites is the story about a magical toy crocodile made out of wax. When it is thrown into water, it turns into a real crocodile! It's a classic story of our times.

KIDS' GAMES

Egyptian children might be tired of grown-ups telling them how young people have things better these days. But it is actually true. Being a kid in Egypt is pretty cool. There are wooden animals to play with, like a toy horse on wheels or a wooden mouse with a tail that goes up and down. Or there are clay balls for playing catch. They are full of seeds so they rattle when you throw them. Even poor children can play with spinning tops moulded out of powdered quartz, which are really cheap to make.

Everybody **needs** good *Neighbours*

Although Egypt is the centre of the ancient world, we're not the only pebble on the beach. There are neighbours all around us. Some have even tried to rule us. So be on your guard for invaders!

Egyptians Invasion ALERT!

Many peoples are jealous of our power and wealth. They are always planning to invade. If you see soldiers in uniforms you don't recognise or who speak a strange language – run! (And tell the authorities.)

Pyramids

The Nubians build their own pyramids – but they keep getting them wrong. They're too tall and steep. They're also a lot smaller than our pyramids. All in all, useless!

Libyans

The semi-nomadic Libyans live northwest of Egypt in the desert. They have dark skin and beards, and blue eyes. They invade often. Libyans once ruled Egypt (the 22nd Dynasty), but they were soon driven out.

THREAT LEVEL ✖ ✖
Irritating, but not really dangerous

Nubians

The Nubians live to the south. These wretches can't even copy our pyramids properly. But they have rich resources. Raids on Nubia bring back gold, ivory and ebony, as well as cattle and prisoners, who make good slaves (despite being wretches!).

THREAT LEVEL ✖ ✖ Virtually a province of Egypt

International shopping list: ✔ Baboons and LIONS from Africa ✔ Cedar from Lebanon

Hyksos

The Hyksos or 'rulers of foreign lands' came from West Asia. They were a violent bunch who established their own dynasty. They brought useful innovations, such as horses, chariots and weapons made from copper. We adopted the innovations – but we got rid of the Hyksos.

THREAT LEVEL ✖ ✖ ✖
Don't harm them and they won't harm you

Sea Peoples

We don't really know who these people were. They came from the Mediterranean coast and were probably fleeing some upheaval. Armies didn't arrive in Egypt alone. They brought their families, their cows and their possessions and settled throughout the Nile Delta.

THREAT LEVEL ✖ ✖ ✖ ✖ ✖
Nearly destroyed Egypt's power

The Romans

We said it would end badly. First Cleopatra had an affair with Julius Caesar, emperor of Rome, and then with Mark Antony. Now Antony has been defeated by Caesar's heir, the emperor Augustus. Cleopatra has killed herself – and Augustus has made Egypt a province of Rome.

THREAT LEVEL ✖ ✖ ✖ ✖ ✖
It's all over! That's the end for us!

Mitanni, Hatti and Assyria

In the New Kingdom we fought wars for 200 years with these neighbouring kingdoms. The wars were over control of Syria. Syria has important trade routes, so it is a great strategic power. We lost many men trying to keep control.

THREAT LEVEL ✖ ✖ ✖ ✖
Don't know when they're beaten

Bring in the New

Have you noticed things are changing in Egypt? Everyone is speaking Greek. And there's a new capital. Alexandria was founded by the Greek king Alexander the Great, who conquered Egypt. Egypt is ruled by a dynasty known as the Ptolemaic Greeks. But Queen Cleopatra seems to be making us more Roman!

Love story
Cleopatra's love for Mark Antony cost them both their lives.

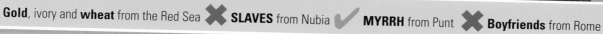

Gold, ivory and **wheat** from the Red Sea ✖ **SLAVES** from Nubia ✔ **MYRRH** from Punt ✖ **Boyfriends** from Rome

Egypt's most
eligible **Bachelor**

Everyone's talking about the new pharaoh! Although only nine, King Tutankhamun is already turning heads. Young girls want to be his queen. Young boys admire his chariot-racing skills.

All washed up
Akhetaten has been covered by the desert sand, The ruins are now called Armana.

Good Pedigree
Ruling is in King Tut's blood. He's the 13th ruler of the remarkable 18th dynasty, which has already included stars such as Thutmose and Hatshepsut.

king **watch**

The boy-king has started well. How could he fail? Everyone hated it when his father, Akhenaten, got rid of all the gods except Amun-Re, or Aten. Tut is not going to make the same mistake. He is bringing back the old gods and restoring the temples and statues his dad damaged. He's also started erasing his father's symbol, or cartouche, everywhere. Akhenaten's capital, Akhetaten at Armana, stands abandoned in the desert.

BOY RACER

King Tut has been making himself unpopular. He races around so quickly in his chariot that he's going to cause an accident. Of course, all pharaohs race chariots. One of the pharaoh's main tasks is to lead the army into battle, so being able to drive a chariot is an essential skill. But really… Our message to our pharaoh is simple: Kill your speed – not yourself!

Inside the **tomb:** **Headrests** Throne, chairs and stools **Charms** against grave **ROBBE**

Obituary

We are sad to confirm the tragic news that Pharaoh Tutankhamun has died aged just 19.

His short reign came to a tragic end yesterday, when the young king was killed in a chariot accident. It's difficult to know exactly what happened, but it seems from the wounds on his leg that he was thrown from his own chariot. Then, while he was trying to pick himself up off the ground, he was struck by another chariot. The injuries he suffered are typical of a road accident.

Queen Ankhesenamun is said to be devastated, especially after the couple's two young daughters were recently stillborn.

A Remarkable Send Off

King Tut's funeral yesterday was remarkable. Thousands of people lined the route to the Valley of the Kings, where pharaohs are now buried (we stopped building pyramids around 1700 B.C.E. – too expensive!). The king was buried with 5,000 precious objects for the Afterlife. Tut wore a gold mask and was buried with treasures including a golden throne and bed, a treasure chest and 413 ushabtis, the wooden figures who will serve the king in the Afterlife.

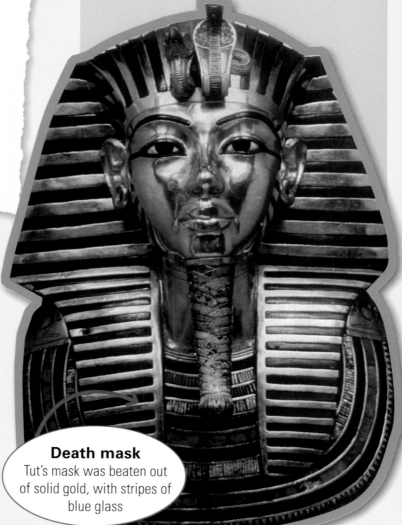

Death mask
Tut's mask was beaten out of solid gold, with stripes of blue glass

SAFETY FIRST

As is usual, the site of King Tut's tomb is going to be a secret, to stop grave robbers from finding it. It will also be protected by the usual magic spells and charms. Anyone who disturbs it will find himself cursed. But what if someone did find it – say, centuries in the future? These three small rooms contain enough treasures to tell people lots about how we Egyptians lived – or how pharaohs lived, anyway.

✔ **Bracelets**, anklets and **EARRINGS** ✔ Crowns ✔ Model **boats** ✘ A mummy's **CURSE**

Glossary

amulet A small charm that protects the wearer against harmful magic.

cartouche An inscription in the shape of an oval shield that identified the names of a pharaoh.

chariot An open-backed two-wheeled vehicle pulled by horses and often used for warfare.

dynasty A family of rulers who pass on power from one to another.

embalmer A person who treats dead bodies in order to preserve them.

inundation A large-scale flood.

hieratic A form of writing that was quicker to write than hieroglyphs.

hieroglyph A picture symbol used in a type of writing. Hieroglyphs could stand for words or sounds.

loincloth A garment made by wrapping a single piece of fabric around the hips.

mineral A naturally occurring substance, such as a metal.

mummy A body that is preserved and wrapped in cloth.

necropolis A large cemetery attached to an ancient city.

Nilometer A scale for measuring the height of the River Nile.

ore A naturally occurring mineral from which metal can be extracted.

papyrus A type of paper made out of reeds.

pharaoh The ruler of Egypt. The title was used mainly in the New Kingdom; earlier rulers were called kings.

scribe Someone who is trained to copy documents.

shaduf A device like a lever for lifting water to a higher level.

silt Fine sand or soil carried by a river and deposited as sediment.

sphinx A creature with a human head and a lion's body, sometimes with wings.

strategic Describes something that is important to a country getting and maintaining long-term power.

tunic A loose, sleeveless garment that reaches to the knees.

On the web

http://www.ancientegypt.co.uk/
Ancient Egypt site maintained by the British Museum.

http://www.bbc.co.uk/history/ancient/egyptians/
BBC site dedicated to the ancient Egyptians.

http://www.childrensuniversity.manchester.ac.uk/interactives/history/egypt/
Interactive ancient Egypt pages from the Children's University of Manchester.

http://www.nms.ac.uk/kids/people_of_the_past/discover_the_egyptians.aspx
The National Museum of Scotland's ancient Egypt pages.

Books

Ancient Egypt (Eyewitness). Dorling Kindersley, 2011.

Caldwell, Stella. *Egyptworld*. Carlton Kids, 2013.

Deary, Terry. *Awful Egyptians* (Horrible Histories). Scholastic, 2013.

Fowke, Bob. *Ancient Egyptians* (What They Don't Tell You About). Wayland, 2013.

Green, Jen. *Ancient Egyptians* (Hail). Wayland, 2013.

Morley, Jacqueline. *You Wouldn't Want to Be a Pyramid Builder* (Hazardous Jobs You'd Rather Not Have). Franklin Watts, 2013.

Powell, Jillian. *Ancient Egyptians* (Craft Box). Wayland, 2013.

Stewart, David. *You Wouldn't Want to Be an Egyptian Mummy* (Disgusting Things You'd Rather Not Know). Franklin Watts, 2012.

Tonge, Neil. *Mangy Mummies, Menacing Pharaohs and Awful Afterlife* (Awfully Ancient). Wayland, 2014.

Tyldesley, Joyce. *Stories from Ancient Egypt*. Oxbow Books, 2013.

Walker, Jane, and Belinda Gallagher. *In Ancient Egypt* (1,000 Facts). Miles Kelly Publishing Ltd., 2006.

Index